Searchlight
BOOKS™

How Does
Government
Work?

Checks and Balances

A Look at the Powers of Government

Kathiann M. Kowalski

Lerner Publications Company
Minneapolis

Lerner Publications Company
A division of Lerner Publishing Group, Inc.
241 First Avenue North
Minneapolis, MN 55401 U.S.A.

Website address: www.lernerbooks.com

Library of Congress Cataloging-in-Publication Data

Kowalski, Kathiann M., 1955–
    Checks and balances: a look at the powers of government / by Kathiann M. Kowalski.
       p. cm. — (Searchlight books™—How does government work?)
    Includes index.
    ISBN 978–0–7613–6515–0 (lib. bdg. : alk. paper)
    1. Separation of powers—United States—Juvenile literature. 2. United States—Politics and government—Juvenile literature. I. Title.
    JK305.K69 2012
    320.473'04—dc22   2010042459

Manufactured in the United States of America
1 – DP – 12/31/11

Contents

Chapter 1

A TROUBLED COUNTRY

In the 1600s, people from Europe settled on the eastern coast of North America. Their settlements were called colonies. Great Britain and its king ruled the colonies. That meant people in the colonies had to obey Britain's laws.

This drawing shows the settlement at the Jamestown Colony in modern-day Virginia. Who ruled the colonies?

People in the colonies didn't like Britain's laws. They wanted freedom. They fought for independence, or self-rule, in the Revolutionary War (1775–1783).

Colonial troops (RIGHT) fight against British troops during one of the first battles of the Revolutionary War.

The colonies won independence. But their troubles weren't over. The first U.S. government had many problems.

This drawing shows members of the first U.S. government, including George Washington (STANDING AT LEFT).

America's first government was based on the Articles of Confederation. This document gave each state a lot of power. But it gave the national government limited power. And most of that power belonged to the congress of the Confederation. This was a group made up of leaders from each state.

The Articles of Confederation was written in 1777.

John Hancock (STANDING AT RIGHT) and other members of congress helped to sort out problems that plagued the U.S. government.

The congress chose the president. But the president didn't have much power. His job was mostly to run meetings for the congress.

Even the congress had little real power. It couldn't collect taxes. States agreed to give the congress some money. But they often paid late or not at all. Without money, the national government couldn't do much.

Time for Change

The government needed fixing. A Virginian named James Madison came up with an idea. He suggested sending delegates to Philadelphia. Delegates are people who make decisions on behalf of others. The delegates would make changes to the Articles. They would make the document better.

Almost everyone agreed with Madison's idea. The delegates' meeting was planned for May 1787.

James Madison suggested the idea for the Philadelphia Convention. Delegates met to make changes to the Articles of Confederation.

George Washington ran the meeting. It went on for four months! The delegates took breaks only to sleep and eat. They talked about problems with the Articles.

By fall, the delegates had agreed on a plan. The plan would give the country a stronger national government. The states would no longer have so much power. The delegates put their plan in writing. They called it the Constitution. The next step was getting states to accept, or ratify, the Constitution.

This painting shows George Washington (STANDING AT RIGHT) **addressing the delegates in Philadelphia.**

Persuading the People

Many people worried about having a stronger national government. They were afraid the new government would take away their rights.

Three political leaders—James Madison, Alexander Hamilton, and John Jay—tried to put people's minds at rest. They wrote letters to newspapers. The letters explained that the government would protect people's rights. The letters also said states' rights would be protected.

James Madison, Alexander Hamilton, and John Jay published the letters they wrote to support the Constitution in a booklet called *The Federalist*.

T H E

FEDERALIST:

A COLLECTION

O F

E S S A Y S,

WRITTEN IN FAVOUR OF THE

NEW CONSTITUTION,

AS AGREED UPON BY THE FEDERAL CONVENTION,
SEPTEMBER 17, 1787.

IN TWO VOLUMES.

VOL. I.

NEW-YORK:

PRINTED AND SOLD BY J. AND A. M'LEAN,
No. 41, HANOVER-SQUARE,
M, DCC, LXXXVIII,

Separation of powers was the key to safeguarding rights. The national government would have three separate parts. The parts would be called branches. The branches would be the legislative branch, the executive branch, and the judicial branch. No one branch would have all the power.

Supreme Court judges (FRONT ROW)—members of the judicial branch—listen to a presidential speech.

The U.S. Capitol Building in Washington, D.C., is where the legislative branch of government meets.

Separation of powers is still an important part of our government. That government has existed for more than two hundred years. It continues to keep the freedoms of Americans safe.

Chapter 2

THE CONGRESS

The government has changed since the late 1700s. It no longer has a group called the congress of the Confederation. But it does have a group simply called the Congress.

Members of Congress gather in 2011. What are the two parts of Congress?

The Congress makes up the legislative branch. It has two parts. They are the Senate and the House of Representatives. Members of the Senate and the House help make laws. Laws are also known as legislation. That's why Congress is called the legislative branch.

Members of the House and the Senate meet to work out legislation.

Keeping the President in Check

The legislative branch helps keep the executive branch in check. That means Congress limits the powers of the executive branch. The president leads the executive branch.

For example, the president chooses people for different jobs. But the Senate must approve many of the president's choices. Sometimes the Senate approves job candidates quickly. Other times, approval takes months. Still other candidates get rejected.

President Barack Obama speaks to reporters at the White House in 2010.

Arizona senator John McCain (RIGHT) and other senators speak to the press in 2011 about approving legislation.

The Constitution gives the president the power to make treaties. Treaties are agreements with other countries. But treaties go into effect only if the Senate approves them. For a treaty to be approved, more than half of all senators must vote to approve it.

Impeachment is Congress's biggest check against the president. Impeachment is the act of charging a public leader with serious wrongdoing. Only the House can decide whether to impeach a president. More than half of the House members must vote to have a president impeached.

Richard Nixon, our thirty-seventh president, left office before the House could impeach him.

Once a president is impeached, the Senate holds a trial. At the trial, the Senate decides whether to convict the president. Conviction removes the president from office. Two-thirds of the senators must vote to convict for the president to be removed.

Bill Clinton, our forty-second president, was impeached. But the Senate, shown here discussing Clinton's impeachment, decided not to convict him.

Chapter 3

THE PRESIDENT AND VETO POWER

The president also keeps Congress in check. Vetoes, or rejections, are one of the president's best tools for keeping Congress in check. Vetoes stop Congress from turning bills (written plans for new laws) into laws. The president vetoes bills that he or she doesn't agree with.

This political cartoon from 1879 shows President Rutherford B. Hayes using his veto power. What do vetoes do?

Vetoes can be overridden (stopped) by Congress. But overriding a veto isn't easy. Once a bill is vetoed, it doesn't usually become a law.

MEMBERS OF THE HOUSE AND THE SENATE CANNOT EASILY OVERRIDE A PRESIDENTIAL VETO.

How Vetoes Work

After the House and the Senate pass a bill, the bill goes to the president. The president gets ten days to sign or veto the bill. If the president signs the bill, it becomes a law. If the president doesn't like a bill, he or she vetoes it.

If the president vetoes the bill, it is returned to Congress. The president also sends along the reasons for vetoing the bill.

President Obama signs a bill while members of the House and Senate watch.

After a veto, Congress reconsiders the bill. Then it votes. If two-thirds of the Senate and the House vote for the bill, Congress overrides the veto. That means the bill becomes law despite the veto.

President Grover Cleveland used his veto power many times while in office. He is shown here in 1892.

President George W. Bush (FIFTH FROM LEFT) meets with leaders of Congress in 2006.

Negotiation

How do laws get passed with veto power in place? What stops presidents from vetoing all Congress's bills? The veto power gets Congress and the president to negotiate. By negotiating, or talking about, their differences, the two sides might come to agree on changes to a bill.

If small changes to a bill can avoid a veto, Congress may compromise. That means it may not get the exact bill it wanted. But Congress gets a law it can take credit for.

The president has reason to negotiate too. The president may need Congress's support for other programs. So presidents often compromise on one bill to get support for another.

President Bill Clinton signs a bill into law in 2000.

Chapter 4

THE COURTS

The judicial branch keeps both Congress and the president in check. The judicial branch is made up of the Supreme Court (the nation's highest court) and other courts.

This 2010 photo shows the nine Supreme Court judges. Which branch of government does the Supreme Court belong to?

The courts' job is to oversee trials. In a trial, a judge decides which laws apply to the disagreement. Then the judge or a jury listens to both sides. They decide which side should win based on the laws.

A judge (CENTER) listens to a witness (LEFT) speaking in a court. The man at right is a lawyer arguing the case before the court.

Sometimes the laws that apply to a disagreement aren't clear. Their meaning may be hard to figure out.

A JUDGE HAS TO APPLY THE
LAW TO EACH CASE THAT
COMES BEFORE THE COURT.

In that case, the Constitution gives the courts power to decide what the laws mean. The courts also have the power to reject laws that go against the Constitution.

Courts often have juries (IN THE BACKGROUND) to make decisions about court cases. Here a lawyer (FRONT LEFT) talks with a client (FRONT RIGHT) during a court case.

President Obama signs a bill while surrounded by members of Congress in 2011. The courts keep the power of the other two branches of government in check.

The courts' power to reject laws limits Congress's power. It limits the president's power too. Congress and the president can make laws. But the courts will not enforce those laws unless they're constitutional.

Keeping Courts in Check

The president and Congress also keep the courts in check. The president picks people to serve as judges in the courts. The Senate votes whether to approve the president's choices. So it's up to the president and the Senate to choose who is part of the Supreme Court.

Elena Kagan (LEFT) is sworn in as a Supreme Court judge in 2010. President Obama picked Kagan for the Court.

Chapter 5

THE STATES AND THE PEOPLE

Government's three branches are important. But they don't have all the power. States have power too. And citizens play the most important role of all. In the end, all parts of government must answer to citizens.

Supporters cheer for a presidential candidate in 2004. What role do citizens have in the U.S. government?

Divided Power

The Constitution divides power between the U.S. government and the states. Some powers belong to just the U.S. government. Others belong to just the states. Still others are shared by the states and the U.S. government.

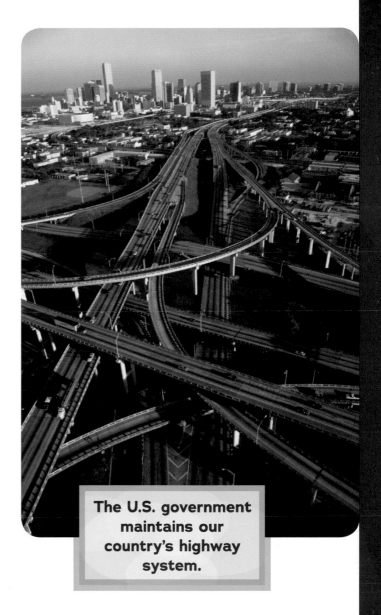

The U.S. government maintains our country's highway system.

What powers belong only to the U.S. government? The power to print money is one. Declaring war is another.

What powers belong only to the states? Only states can give licenses for driving and getting married. Only states can set rules for practicing professions such as law or medicine.

Money in the United States can be printed only by the U.S. government.

Powers shared by the U.S. government and the states include protecting the environment. The Environmental Protection Agency is run by the U.S. government. It sets standards for keeping the air, land, and water clean. But the states run programs to meet those standards.

Two workers check for materials that could harm the environment.

People Power

What powers do citizens have? Citizens choose the president by voting. They vote for senators and other officials too.

Citizens not old enough to vote also have power. Young people can learn about political issues. They can write the president about issues that concern them.

Voting is a powerful right for citizens of the United States.

Being an American citizen is a privilege. It's also a responsibility. The preamble (introduction) to the Constitution refers to "the blessings of liberty." Do your part to ensure these blessings for all Americans.

These young citizens pick up trash in Detroit, Michigan. Keeping your neighborhood clean is one way to help out and be responsible.

Glossary

bill: a written plan for a new law

citizen: a person who lives in a city, a state, or a country

colony: a territory that has been settled by people from another country and is controlled by another country

Congress: a group of elected officials who write, talk about, and make laws. The U.S. Congress is made up of the Senate and the House of Representatives.

delegate: someone who represents other people at a meeting

executive branch: the branch of government that is led by the president

impeachment: the act of charging a public leader with serious wrongdoing

judicial branch: the branch of government involving the court system

legislation: laws

legislative branch: the branch of government that makes laws

negotiate: to discuss something until you reach agreement

override: to cancel or stop

tax: money that people and businesses must pay to support a government

treaty: an agreement with another nation

veto: to reject a bill and keep it from becoming a law

Learn More about Government

Books

Hamilton, John. *Branches of Government*. Edina, MN: Abdo, 2005. Hamilton tells all about the three branches that make up our government.

Stier, Catherine. *If I Ran for President*. Morton Grove, IL: Albert Whitman, 2007. Six children explain the election process and its importance in this lively book.

Swain, Gwenyth. *Documents of Freedom: A Look at the Declaration of Independence, the Bill of Rights, and the U.S. Constitution*. Minneapolis: Lerner Publications Company, 2012. This informative title explores the Declaration of Independence, the Constitution, and the Bill of Rights—three documents that act as road maps for our country's government.

Thomas, William David. *What Are the Parts of Government?* Pleasantville, NY: Gareth Stevens, 2008. This selection discusses the three parts of government and how they balance one another.

Websites

Ben's Guide to U.S. Government for Kids
http://bensguide.gpo.gov/3-5/index.html
This useful website is full of information about the U.S. government and how it works.

The Democracy Project
http://pbskids.org/democracy
This site lets you fill out a job application to be president for a day, send e-cards to adults reminding them to vote, and print political stickers designed by students.

United States Government for Kids
http://library.thinkquest.org/5873
Visit this page designed by students to read all about the government, its branches, and more.

Index

Photo Acknowledgments

The images in this book are used with the permission of: © Bettman/CORBIS, pp. 4, 5, 8
© PoodlesRock/CORBIS, p. 6; National Archives (ARC Identifier 301687), p. 7; Library of Congress
pp. 9 (LC-DIG-ppmsca-19166), 20 (LC-USZC2-1239); © SuperStock, p. 10; © FotoSearch/Stringer/
Archive Photos/Getty Images, p. 11; © Owen Franken/CORBIS, p. 12; © Phil Degginger/Alamy, p. 13; ©
Jim Lo Scalzo/epa/CORBIS, p. 14; © Scott J. Ferrell/Congressional Quarterly/Getty Images, pp. 15, 19;
© Alex Wong/Getty Images, p. 16; © Chip Somodevilla/Getty Images, pp. 17, 21, 26; AP Photo,
p. 18; © Mark Wilson/Getty Images, pp. 22, 24; © CORBIS, p. 23; © Mark Wilson/Newsmakers/Getty
Images, p. 25; © PNC/Photodisc/Getty Images, p. 27; © Bart Ah You-Pool/Getty Images, p. 28;
© Stockbyte/Getty Images, p. 29; © Brendan Smialowski/Bloomberg via Getty Images, p. 30;
© J. Scott Applewhite/Pool/CNP/CORBIS, p. 31; © Jeff Greenberg/Alamy, p. 32; © Nomad/SuperStock,
p. 33; © Purestock/Getty Images, p. 34; © Cusp/SuperStock, p. 35; © Logan Mock-Bunting/Stringer/
Getty Images, p. 36; © imagebroker.net/SuperStock, p. 37.
Front Cover: © Ken Skalski/CORBIS (left); © Ambient Ideas/Shutterstock Images (top/right); © Saul
Loeb/AFP/Getty Images (middle/right); © Chip Somodevilla/Getty Images (bottom/right).

Main body text set in Adrianna Regular 14/20
Typeface provided by Chank